THE

CHRISTIAN SCHOLARSHIP

J. GRESHAM MACHEN

SHELTON COLLEGE PRESS
CAPE MAY, N.J.
1932

CROSSREACH
PUBLICATIONS

Hope. Inspiration. Trust.

WE'RE SOCIAL! FOLLOW US FOR NEW TITLES AND DEALS:
FACEBOOK.COM/CROSSREACHPUBLICATIONS
@CROSSREACHPUB

AVAILABLE IN PAPERBACK AND EBOOK EDITIONS

PLEASE GO ONLINE FOR MORE GREAT TITLES
AVAILABLE THROUGH CROSSREACH PUBLICATIONS.
AND IF YOU ENJOYED THIS BOOK PLEASE CONSIDER LEAVING A
REVIEW ON AMAZON. THAT HELPS US OUT A LOT. THANKS.

CONTENTS

THE IMPORTANCE OF CHRISTIAN SCHOLARSHIP[1]

INTRODUCTION

IT SEEMS TO ME, as I stand here before you today, that there is one blessing in these days of defection and unbelief which we have come to value as we never valued it before. That is the blessing of Christian fellowship in the presence of a hostile world, and in the presence of a visible Church which too often has departed from the Word of God. Today, during the three meetings of this League, in the portion of the meetings which has been allotted to me, I am to have the privilege of delivering three addresses on the subject, "The Importance of Christian Scholarship."

It is no doubt unfortunate that the person who speaks about this subject should have so limited an experimental acquaintance with the subject about which he is endeavoring to speak; but in

---

[1] This article contains three lectures given at meetings of the Bible League in Caxton Hall, Westminster, London on June 17, 1932. Originally published by Shelton College Press, Cape May, N.J.

these days of anti-intellectualism you may be willing to hear a word in defense of the intellect, even from one whose qualifications for speaking on that subject are so limited as mine.

There was a time when the raising of the question as to the importance of Christian scholarship might have seemed to be ridiculous; there was a time when a man who does so much talking as a minister or a Sunday School teacher ought to do, in the propagation of the Faith to which he adheres, would have regarded it as a matter of course that he ought to know something about the subject of which he undertakes to talk.

MODERN TEACHING

But in recent years we have got far beyond all such elementary considerations as that; modern pedagogy has emancipated us, whether we be in the pulpit or in the professor's chair or in the pew, from anything so irksome as earnest labor in the acquisition of knowledge. It never seems to occur to many modern teachers that the primary business of the teacher is to study the subject that he is going to teach. Instead of studying the subject that he is going to teach, he studies "education"; a knowledge of the methodology of teaching takes the place of a knowledge of the particular branch of literature, history or science to which a man has devoted his life.

This substitution of methodology for content in the preparation of the teacher is based upon a particular view of what education is. It is based upon the view that education consists primarily, not in the imparting of information, but in a training of the faculties of the child; that the business of the teacher is not to teach, but to develop in the child a faculty which will enable the child to learn.

This child-centered notion of education seems to involve emancipation from a vast amount of drudgery. It used to be thought necessary to do some hard work at school. When a textbook was given to a class, it was expected that the contents of the textbook should be mastered. But now all that has been changed. Storing up facts in the mind was a long and painful process, and it is indeed comforting to know that we can now do without it. Away with all drudgery and all hard work! Self-expression has taken their place. A great pedagogic discovery has been made–the discovery that it is possible to think with a completely empty mind.

It cannot be said that the results of the discovery are impressive. This child-centered notion of education has resulted, particularly in America, where it has been most ruthlessly applied, in a boundless superficiality of which we Americans certainly have little reason to be proud; but it has probably not been confined to America by any means. I wonder when we shall have that revival of learning which we so much need, and which I verily believe might be, in the providence of God, as was the Renaissance of the fifteenth century, the precursor of a Reformation in the Church. When that revival of learning comes, we may be sure that it will sweep away the present absurd over-emphasis upon methodology in teaching at the expense of content. We shall never have a true revival of learning until teachers turn their attention away from the mere mental process of the child, out into the marvelous richness and variety of the universe and of human life. Not teachers who have studied the methodology of teaching, but teachers who are on fire with a love of the subjects that they are going to teach are the real torch-bearers of intellectual advance.

"RELIGIOUS EDUCATION"

Certainly the present view of education is, when it is applied to the work of the preacher and of the teacher in the Church, skeptical to the core. It is summed up in what is called "religious education." I wonder sometimes at the readiness with which Christian people–I do not mean Church-members, but real Bible-believing Christians–use that term; for the ordinary implications of the term are quite opposed to Christian religion. The fundamental notion underlying the ordinary use of the term "religious education" is that the business of the teacher in the Church is not to impart knowledge of a fixed body of truth which God has revealed, but to train the religious faculty of the child. The religious faculty of the child, it is supposed, may be trained by the use of the most widely diverse doctrinal content; it may be trained in this generation, perhaps, by the thought of a personal God; but in another generation it may be trained equally well by the thought of an ideal humanity as the only God there is. Thus the search for objective and permanent truth is given up, and instead we have turned our attention to the religious faculties of man. In other words, men have become interested today in religion because they have ceased to believe in God.

As over against such skepticism, the Bible, from Genesis to Revelation, presents a body of truth which God has revealed; and if we hold the Biblical view, we shall regard it as our supreme function,

as teachers as well as preachers and as Christian parents and as simple Christians, to impart a knowledge of that body of truth. The Christian preacher, we shall hold, needs above all to know the thing that he is endeavoring to preach.

But if knowledge is necessary to preaching, it does seem probable that the fuller the knowledge is, the better the preacher will be able to do his work. Underlying preaching, in other words, is Christian scholarship; and it is in defense of Christian scholarship that I have thought it might be fitting to say a few words to you today.

Christian scholarship is necessary to the preacher, and to the man who in whatever way, in public or in private, endeavors to proclaim the gospel to his fellow-men, in at least three ways.

I. THE IMPORTANCE OF CHRISTIAN SCHOLARSHIP FOR EVANGELISM

IN THE FIRST PLACE, it is necessary for evangelism. In saying so, I am perfectly well aware of the fact that I am putting myself squarely in conflict with a method of religious work which is widely prevalent at the present time. Knowledge, the advocates of that method seem to think, is quite unnecessary to faith; at the beginning a man may be a Fundamentalist or a Modernist, he may hold a Christian or antiChristian view of Christ. Never mind; he is to be received, quite apart from his opinions, on the basis of simple faith. Afterwards, indeed, he will, if he has really been converted, read his Bible and come to a more and more correct view of Christ and of the meaning of Christ's death. If he does not come to a more and more correct view, one may perhaps suspect that his conversion was not a real one after all. But at the beginning all that is thought to be unnecessary. All that a man has to believe in at the beginning is conversion: he is saved on the basis of simple faith; correct opinions about God and Christ come later.

With regard to this method, it may of course be said at once that the "simple faith" thus spoken of is not faith at all; or, rather, it is not faith in Christ. A man cannot trust a person whom he holds to be untrustworthy. Faith always contains an intellectual element. A very little knowledge is often sufficient if a man is to believe, but some knowledge there must be. So if a man is to trust Christ he must know something about Christ; he may know only a very little, but without some knowledge he could not believe at all.

What these advocates of a "simple faith" which involves no knowledge of Christ really mean by "simple faith" is faith, perhaps, but it is not faith in Christ. It is faith in the practitioners of the method; but it is not faith in Christ. To have faith in Christ one must have knowledge of Christ, however slight; and it is not a matter of indifference whether the opinions held about Christ are true or false.

NEW TESTAMENT EVANGELISM

But is this modern anti-intellectualistic view of faith in accordance with the New Testament? Does the New Testament offer a man salvation first, on the basis of a psychological process of conversion or surrender–falsely called faith–and then preach the gospel to him afterwards; or does the New Testament preach the gospel to him first, set forth to him first the fact about Christ and the meaning of His death, and then ask him to accept the One thus presented in order that his soul may be saved?

That question can be answered very simply by an examination of the examples of conversion which the New Testament contains.

PENTECOST

Three thousand were converted on the day of Pentecost. They were converted by Peter's sermon. What did Peter's sermon contain? Did it contain merely an account of Peter's own experience of salvation; did it consist solely in exhortation to the people to confess their sins? Not at all. What Peter did on the day of Pentecost was to set forth the facts about Jesus Christ–His life, His miracles, His death, His resurrection. It was on the basis of that setting forth of the facts about Christ that the three thousand believed, confessed their sins, and were saved.

PHILIPPI

Paul and Silas were in prison one night at Philippi. There was a miracle; the prisoners were released. The jailer was impressed and said, "What must I do to be saved?" Paul and Silas said: "Believe on the Lord Jesus Christ, and thou shalt be saved." Did the jailer believe then and there; was he saved without further delay? I think not. We are expressly told that Paul and Silas, after that, "spake unto him the word of the Lord." Then and not till then was he baptised, and I think we are plainly to understand that then and not till then was he saved.

CHRIST AND THE WOMAN OF SAMARIA

Our Savior sat one day by the well. He talked with a sinful woman, and laid His finger upon the sore spot in her life. "Thou has had five husbands." He said; "and he whom thou now hast is not thy husband." The woman then apparently sought to evade the consideration of the sin in her own life by asking a theological question regarding the right place in which to worship God. What did Jesus do with her theological question? Did He brush it aside after the manner of modern religious workers? Did He say to the woman: "You are evading the real question; do not trouble yourself about theological matters, but let us return to the consideration of sin in your life?" Not at all. He answered that theological question with the utmost fullness as though the salvation of the woman's soul depended on her obtaining the right answer. In reply to that sinful woman, and to what modern religious workers would have regarded as an evasive question, Jesus engaged in some of the profoundest theological teaching in the whole New Testament. A right view of God, according to Jesus, is not something that comes after salvation, but it is something necessary to salvation.

PAUL'S MISSIONARY PREACHING

The Apostle Paul in the First Epistle to the Thessalonians gives a precious summary of his missionary preaching. He does so by telling what it was to which the Thessalonians turned when they were saved.

Was it a mere program of life to which they turned? Was it a "simple faith," in the modern sense which divorces faith from knowledge and supposes that a man can have "simple faith" in a person of whom he knows nothing or about whom he holds opinions that make faith in him absurd? Not at all. In turning to Christ those

Thessalonian Christians turned to a system of theology. "Ye turned to God from idols," says Paul, "to serve the living and true God; and to wait for His Son from heaven, whom He raised from the dead, even Jesus, which delivereth us from the wrath to come." "Ye turned to God from idols"–there is theology proper. "And to wait for His Son from heaven"–there is Christology. "Whom He raised from the dead"– there is the supernatural act of God in history. "Even Jesus"–there is the humanity of our Lord. "Which delivereth us from the wrath to come"– there is the Christian doctrine of sin and the Christian doctrine of the Cross of Christ.

So it is in the New Testament from beginning to end. The examples might be multiplied indefinitely. The New Testament gives not one bit of comfort to those who separate faith from knowledge, to those who hold the absurd view that a man can trust a person about whom he knows nothing. What many men despise today as "doctrine" the New Testament calls the gospel; and the New Testament treats it as the message upon which salvation depends.

But if that be so, if salvation depends upon the message in which Christ is offered as Savior, it is obviously important that we should get the message straight. That is where Christian scholarship comes in. Christian scholarship is important in order that we may tell the story of Jesus and His love straight and full and plain.

THE SIMPLICITY OF THE GOSPEL!

At this point, indeed, an objection may arise. Is not the gospel a very simple thing, it may be asked; and will not its simplicity be obscured by too much scholarly research? The objection spring from a false view of what scholarship is; it springs from the notion that scholarship leads a man to be obscure. Exactly the reverse is the case. Ignorance is obscure; but scholarship brings order out of confusion, places things in their logical relations, and makes the message shine forth clear.

There are, indeed, evangelists who are not scholars, but scholarship is necessary to evangelism all the same. In the first place, though there are evangelists, who are not scholars, the greatest evangelists, like the Apostle Paul and like Martin Luther, have been scholars. In the second place, the evangelists who are not scholars are dependent upon scholars to help them get their message straight; it is out of a great underlying fund of Christian learning that true evangelism springs.

LIFE FOUNDED ON TRUTH

That is something that the Church of our day needs to take to heart. Life, according to the New Testament, is founded upon truth; and the attempt to reverse the order results only in despair and in spiritual death. Let us not deceive ourselves, my friends. Christian experience is necessary to evangelism; but evangelism does not consist merely in the rehearsal of what has happened in the evangelist's own soul. We shall, indeed, be but poor witnesses of Christ if we can tell only what Christ has done for the world or for the Church and cannot tell what He has done personally for us. But we shall also be poor witnesses if we recount only the experiences of our own lives. Christian evangelism does not consist merely in a man's going about the world saying: "Look at me, what a wonderful experience I have, how happy I am, what wonderful Christian virtues I exhibit; you can all be as good and as happy as I am if you will just make a complete surrender of your wills in obedience to what I say." That is what many religious workers seem to think that evangelism is. We can preach the gospel, they tell us, by our lives, and do not need to preach it by our words. But they are wrong. *Men are not saved by the exhibition of our glorious Christian virtues*; they are not saved by the contagion of our experiences. We cannot be the instruments of God in saving them if we preach to them thus only ourselves. Nay, we must preach to them the Lord Jesus Christ; for it is only through the gospel which sets Him forth that they can be saved.

HOW TO BE SAVED

If you want health for your souls, and if you want to be the instrument of bringing health to others, do not turn your gaze forever within, as though you could find Christ there. Nay, turn your gaze away from your own miserable experiences, away from your own sin, to the Lord Jesus Christ as He is offered to us in the gospel. "As Moses lifted up the serpent in the wilderness, even so must the Son of Man be lifted up." Only when we turn away from ourselves to that uplifted Savior shall we have healing for our deadly hurt. It is the same old story, my friends—the same old story of the natural man. Men are trying today, as they have always been trying, to save themselves–to save themselves by their own act of surrender, by the excellence of their own faith, by mystic experiences of their own lives. But it is all in vain. Not that way is peace with God to be obtained. It is to be obtained only in the old, old way–by attention to something that was done once for all long ago, and by acceptance of the living Savior who there, once for all, brought redemption for our sin. Oh, that men would turn for salvation from their own experience to the Cross of Christ; oh, that they would *turn from the phenomena of religion to the living God!*

That that may be done, there is but one way. It is not found in a study of the psychology of religion; it is not found in "religious education"; it is not found in an analysis of one's' own spiritual states. Oh, no. It is found only in the blessed written Word. There are the words of life. There God speaks. Let us attend to His voice. Let us above all things know the Word. Let us study it with all our minds, let us cherish it with all our hearts. Then let us try, very humbly, to bring it to the unsaved. Let us pray that God may honor not the messengers but the message, that despite our unworthiness He may make His Word upon our unworthy lips to be a message of life.

II. THE IMPORTANCE OF CHRISTIAN SCHOLARSHIP FOR THE DEFENSE OF THE FAITH

IN SPEAKING OF CHRISTIAN SCHOLARSHIP before the Bible League, I am somewhat in the position of bringing coals to Newcastle, but perhaps you will take what I am saying as being an expression of

hearty agreement with that scholarly work which your League has been carrying on so successfully for many years. This morning we considered the importance of Christian scholarship for evangelists. The gospel message, we observed, is not brought to a man after salvation has already been received, but it is brought to him in order that salvation may be received; and the fuller and plainer the message is, so much the more effective is it for the saving of souls.

THE NEED FOR THE DEFENSE OF THE FAITH

But Christian scholarship is also necessary, in the second place, for the defense of the faith, and to this aspect of the subject I invite your attention this afternoon. There are, indeed, those who tell us that no defense of the faith is necessary. "The Bible needs no defense," they say; "let us not be forever defending Christianity, but instead let us go forth joyously to propagate Christianity." But I have observed one curious fact–when men talk thus about propagating Christianity without defending it, the thing that they are propagating is pretty sure not to be Christianity at all. They are propagating an antiintellectualistic, non-doctrinal Modernism; and the reason why it requires no defense is simply that it is so completely in accord with the current of the age. It causes no more disturbance than does a chip that floats downward with a stream. In order to be an adherent of it, a man does not need to resist anything at all: he needs only to drift, and automatically his Modernism will be of the most approved and popular kind. One thing needs always to be remembered in the Christian Church–*true Christianity, now as always, is radically contrary to the natural man*, and it cannot possibly be maintained without a constant struggle. A chip that floats downwards with the current is always at peace; but around every rock the waters foam and rage. Show me a professing Christian of whom all men speak well, and I will show you a man who is probably unfaithful to his Lord.

THE IMPORTANCE OF ARGUMENT

Certainly a Christianity that avoids argument is not the Christianity of the New Testament. The New Testament is full of argument in defense of the faith. The Epistles of Paul are full of argument—no

one can doubt that. But even the words of Jesus are full of argument in defense of the truth of what Jesus was saying. "If ye then, being evil, know how to give good gifts unto your children, how much more shall your Father which is in heaven give good things to them that ask Him?" Is not that a well-known form of reasoning, which the logicians would put in its proper category? Many of the parables of Jesus are argumentative in character. Even our Lord, who spake in the plenitude of divine authority, did condescend to reason with men. Everywhere the New Testament meets objections fairly, and presents the gospel as a thoroughly reasonable thing.

Some years ago I was in a company of students who were discussing methods of Christian work.

An older man, who had had much experience in working among students, arose and said that according to his experience you never win a man to Christ until you stop arguing with him. When he said that, I was not impressed.

It is perfectly true, of course, that argument alone is quite insufficient to make a man a Christian. You may argue with him from now until the end of the world: you may bring forth the most magnificent arguments: but all will be in vain unless there be one other thing–the mysterious, creative power of the Holy Spirit in the new birth. But because argument is insufficient, it does not follow that it is unnecessary. Sometimes it is used directly by the Holy Spirit to bring a man to Christ. But more frequently it is used indirectly. A man hears an answer to objections raised against the truth of the Christian religion: and at the time when he hears it he is not impressed. But afterwards, perhaps many years afterwards, his heart at last is touched: he is convicted of sin; he desires to be saved. Yet without that half-forgotten argument he could not believe: the gospel would not seem to him to be true, and he would remain in his sin. As it is, however, the thought of what he has heard long ago comes into his mind; Christian apologetics at last has its day, the way is open, and when he will believe he can believe because he has been made to see that believing is not an offence against truth.

THE PLACE OF CHRISTIAN APOLOGETICS TODAY

Sometimes, when I have tried–very imperfectly, I confess–to present arguments in defense of the resurrection of our Lord or of

the truth, at this point or that, of God's Word, someone has come up to me after the lecture and has said to me very kindly: "We liked it, and we are impressed with the considerations that you have adduced in defense of the faith; but, the trouble is, we all believed in the Bible already, and the persons that really needed the lecture are not here." When someone tells me that, I am not very greatly disturbed. True, I should have liked to have just as many skeptics as possible at my lecture; but if they are not there I do not necessarily think that my efforts are all in vain. What I am trying to do by my apologetic lecture is not merely–perhaps not even primarily–to convince people who are opposed to the Christian religion. Rather am I trying to give to Christian people–Christian parents or Sunday

School teachers–materials that they can use not in dealing with avowed skeptics, whose backs are up against Christianity, but in dealing with their own children or with the pupils in their classes, who love them, and long to be Christians as they are, but are troubled by the hostile voices on every side.

It is but a narrow view of Christian apologetics that regards the defense of the faith as being useful only in the immediate winning of those who are arguing vigorously on the other side. Rather is it useful most of all in producing an intellectual atmosphere in which the acceptance of the gospel will seem to be something other than an offence against truth. Charles Spurgeon and D. L. Moody, in the latter years of the nineteenth century, were facing a situation entirely different from that which faces the evangelists of today: They were facing a world in which many people in their youth had been imbued with Christian convictions, and in which public opinion, to a very considerable extent, was in favor of the Christian faith. Today, on the other hand, public opinion, even in England and America, is predominantly opposed to the Christian faith, and the people from their youth are imbued with the notion that Christian convictions are antiquated and absurd. *Never was there a stronger call of God than there is today for a vigorous and scholarly defense of the faith.*

I believe that the more thoughtful of the evangelists are coming to recognize that fact. There was a time, twenty-five or thirty years ago, when the evangelists regarded the work of Christian apologists as either impious or a waste of time. Here are souls to be saved, they said; and professors in theological seminaries insist on confusing their students' minds with a lot of German names, instead of preaching the simple gospel of Christ. But today a different temper often prevails. Evangelists, if they be real evangelists, real proclaimers of the unpopular message that the Bible contains, are coming more and more to see that they cannot do without those despised theological professors after all. It is useless to proclaim a gospel that people cannot hold to be true: no amount of emotional appeal can do anything against the truth. *The question of fact cannot permanently be evaded.* Did Christ or did He not rise from the dead: is the Bible trustworthy or is it false? In other words, the twelfth chapter of I. Corinthians is coming again to its rights. We are coming to understand how manysided is the work of Christ: the eye is ceasing to "say to the hand, 'I have no need of thee.'" "Certainly one thing is clear—if Christian apologetics suffers, injury will *come to every member* of the body of Christ.

But if we are to have Christian apologetics, if we are to have a defense of the faith, what kind of defense of the faith should it be?

CONTROVERSY IN THE CHURCH

In the first place, it should be directed not only against the opponents outside the Church but also against the opponents within. The opponents of Holy Scripture do not become less dangerous, but they become far more dangerous when they are within ecclesiastical walls. At that point, I am well aware that widespread objection arises at the present time. Let us above all, men say, have no controversy in the Church: let us forget our small theological differences and all repeat together Paul's hymn to Christian love. As I listen to such pleas, my Christian friends, I think I can detect in them rather plainly the voice of Satan. That voice is heard, sometimes, on the lips of good and truly Christian men, as at Caesarea Philippi it was heard on the lips of the greatest of the Twelve. But Satan's voice it is, all the same.

Sometimes it comes to us in rather deceptive ways.

I remember, for example, what was said in my hearing on one occasion, by a man who is generally regarded as one of the leaders of the evangelical Christian Church. It was said at the climax of a day of devotional services. "If you go heresy-hunting for the sin in your own wicked hearts," said the speaker, as nearly as I can remember his words, "you will have no time for heresy-hunting for the heretics outside."

Thus did temptation come through the mouth of a well-meaning man. The "heretics," to use the term that was used by that speaker, are, with their helpers, the indifferentists, in control of the church within the bounds of which that utterance was made, the Presbyterian Church in the United States of America, as they are in control of nearly all the larger Protestant churches in the world. A man hardly needs to "hunt" them very long if he is to oppose them. All that he needs to do is to be faithful to the Lord Jesus Christ, and his opposition to those men will follow soon enough.

But is it true, as this speaker seemed to imply, *that there is a conflict between faithfulness to Christ in the ecclesiastical world and the cultivation of holiness in one's own inner life?* My friends, it is not true, but false. A man cannot successfully go heresy-hunting against the sin in his own life if he is willing to deny his Lord in the presence of the enemies outside. The two battles are intimately connected. A man cannot fight successfully in one unless he fights also in the other.

PRAYER AND THEOLOGICAL DIFFERENCES

Again, we are told that our theological differences will disappear if we will just get down on our knees together in prayer. Well, I can only say about that kind of prayer, which is indifferent to the question whether the gospel is true or false, that it is not Christian prayer; it is bowing down in the house of Rimmon. God save us from it! Instead, may God lead us to the kind of prayer in which, recognizing the dreadful condition of the visible Church, recognizing the unbelief and the sin which dominate it today, we who are opposed to the current of the age both in the world and in the Church, facing the facts as they are, lay those facts before God, as Hezekiah laid before Him the threatening letter of the Assyrian enemy, and humbly ask Him to give the answer.

CONTROVERSY AND REVIVAL

Again, men say that instead of engaging in controversy in the Church, we ought to pray to God for a revival; instead of polemics, we ought

to have evangelism. Well, what kind of revival do you think that will be? What sort of evangelism is it that is indifferent to the question what evangel is it that is to be preached? Not a revival in the New Testament sense, not the evangelism that Paul meant when he said, "Woe is be unto me, if I preach not the gospel." No, my friends, there can be no true evangelism which makes common cause with the enemies of the Cross of Christ. Souls will hardly be saved unless the evangelists can say with Paul: "If we or an angel from heaven preach any other gospel than that which we preached unto you, let him be accursed!" Every true revival is born in controversy, and leads to more controversy. That has been true ever since our Lord said that He came not to bring peace upon the earth but a sword. And do you know what I think will happen when God sends a new Reformation upon the Church? We cannot tell when that blessed day will come. But when the blessed day does come, I think we can say at least one result that it will bring. We shall hear nothing on that day about the evils of controversy in the Church. All that will be swept away as with a mighty flood. A man who is on fire with a message never talks in that wretched, feeble way, but proclaims the truth joyously and fearlessly, in the presence of every high thing that is lifted up against the gospel of Christ.

THE HOLY SPIRIT AND DOCTRINE

But men tell us that instead of engaging in controversy about doctrine we ought to seek the power of the living Holy Spirit. A few years ago we had in America, as I suppose you had here, a celebration of the anniversary of Pentecost. At that time, our Presbyterian Church was engaged in a conflict, the gist of which concerned the question of the truth of the Bible. Was the Church going to insist, or was it not going to insist, that its ministers should believe that the Bible is true? At that time of decision, and almost, it seemed, as though to evade the issue. Many sermons were preached on the subject of the Holy Spirit. Do you think that those sermons, if they really were preached in that way, were approved by Him with whom they dealt? I fear not, my friends. A man can hardly receive the power of the Holy Spirit if he seeks to evade the question whether the blessed Book that the Spirit has given us is true or false.

POSITIVE PREACHING!

Again, men tell us that our preaching should be positive and not negative, that we can preach the truth without attacking error. But if we follow that advice we shall have to close our Bible and desert its teachings. The New Testament is a polemic book almost from beginning to end. Some years ago I was in a company of teachers of the Bible in the colleges and other educational institutions of America. One of the most eminent theological professors in the country made an address. In it he admitted that there are unfortunate controversies about doctrine in the Epistles of Paul; but, said he in effect, the real essence of Paul's teaching is found in the hymn to Christian love in the thirteenth chapter of I Corinthians: and we can avoid controversy today, if we will only devote the chief attention to that inspiring hymn. In reply, I am bound to say that the example was singularly ill-chosen. That hymn to Christian love is in the midst of a great polemic passage: it would never have been written if Paul had been opposed to controversy with error in the Church. It was because his soul was stirred within him by a wrong use of the spiritual gifts that he was able to write that glorious hymn. So it is always in the Church. Every really great Christian utterance, it may almost be said, is born in controversy. It is when men have felt compelled to take a stand against error, that they have risen to the really great heights in the celebration of truth.

THE METHOD OF DEFENSE

But in defending the faith against the attack upon it that is being made both without and within the Church, what method of defense should be used? In answer to that question, I have time only to say two things. In the first place, the defense, with the polemic that it involves, should be perfectly open and above board. I have just stated, that I believe in controversy. But in controversy I do try to observe the Golden Rule; I do try to do unto others as I would have others do unto me. And the kind of controversy that pleases me in an opponent is a controversy that is altogether frank.

Sometimes I go into a company of modern men. A man gets up upon the platform, looks out benignly upon the audience, and says: "I think, brethren, that we are all agreed about this"–and then proceeds to trample ruthlessly upon everything that is dearest to my heart. When he does that, I feel aggrieved. I do not feel aggrieved because he gives free expression to opinions that are different from mine. But I feel aggrieved because he calls me his "brother" and assumes, prior to investigation, that I agree with what he is going to say. A kind of controversy that pleases me better than that is a kind of controversy in which a man gets up upon the platform, looks out upon the audience. and says: "What is this? I see that one of those absurd Fundamentalists has somehow strayed into this company of educated men"–and then proceeds to call me by every opprobrious term that is to be found in one of the most unsavory paragraphs of Roget's "Thesaurus." When he does that, I do not feel too much distressed. I can even endure that application to me of the term "Fundamentalist," though for the life of me I cannot see why adherents of the Christian religion, which has been in the world for some nineteen hundred years, should suddenly be made an "-ism," and be called by some strange new name. The point is that that speaker at least does me the honor of recognizing that a profound difference separates my view from his. We understand each other perfectly, and it is quite possible that we may be, if not brothers (I object to the degradation of that word), yet at least good friends.

A SCHOLARLY DEFENSE OF THE FAITH

In the second place, the defense of the faith should be of a scholarly kind. Mere denunciation does not constitute an argument; and before a man can refute successfully an argument of an opponent, he must understand the argument that he is endeavoring to refute. Personalities, in such debate, should be kept in the background; and analysis of the motives of one's opponents has little place. That principle, certainly in America, has been violated constantly by the advocates of the Modernist or indifferentist position in the Church. It has been violated by them far more than by the defenders of God's Word. Yet the latter, strangely enough, have received the blame. The representatives of the dominant Modern-indifferentist forces have engaged in the most violent adjectival abuse of their opponents: yet they have been called sweet and beautiful and tolerant: the defenders of the Bible, and of the historic position of the Church have spoken courteously, though plainly, in opposition, and have been called "bitter" and "extreme." I am reminded of the way in which an intelligent American Indian is reported (I saw it in the American magazine, "The Saturday Evening Post," a few months ago) to have characterized the terminology used in histories of the wars between the white men and the men of his race. "When you won," said the Indian, "it was, according to your histories, a 'battle'; when we won, it was a 'massacre.'"

Such, I suppose, is the treatment of the unpopular side in every conflict. Certainly it is the treatment which we receive today. Men have found it to be an effective way of making themselves popular, to abuse the representatives of so unpopular a cause as that which we Bible-believing Christians represent.

Yet I do not think we ought to be dismayed. If in these days of unbelief and defection in the Church we are called upon to bear just a little bit of the reproach of Christ, we ought to count ourselves honored, and certainly we ought not to mitigate in the slightest measure the plainness either of our defense of the truth or of our warnings against error. Men's favor is worth very little after all, in comparison with the favor of Christ.

But certainly we should strive to keep ourselves free from that with which we are charged. Because our opponents are guilty, that is no reason why we should make ourselves guilty too.

KNOWLEDGE OF TRUTH AND ERROR

It is no easy thing to defend the Christian faith against the mighty attack that is being brought against it at the present day. Knowledge of the truth is necessary, and also clear acquaintance with the forces hostile to the truth in modern thought.

At that point, a final objection may arise. Does it not involve a terrible peril to men's souls to ask them—for example, in their preparation for the ministry—to acquaint themselves with things that are being said against the gospel of the Lord Jesus Christ? Would it not be safer to learn only of the truth, without acquainting ourselves with error? We answer, "Of course it would be safer." It would be far safer, no doubt, to live in a fool's paradise and close one's eyes to what is going on in the world today, just as it is safer to remain in secure dugouts rather than to go over the top in some great attack. We save our souls, perhaps, by such tactics, but the Lord's enemies remain in possession of the field. It is a great battle indeed, this intellectual battle of today; deadly perils await every man who engages in that conflict; but it is the Lord's battle, and He is a great Captain in the fight.

There are, indeed, some perils that should be avoided–particularly the peril of acquainting ourselves with what is said against the Christian religion without ever obtaining any really orderly acquaintance with what can be said for it. That is the peril to which a candidate for the ministry, for example, subjects himself when he attends only one of the theological colleges where the professors are adherents of the dominant naturalistic view. What does such a course of study mean? It means simply this, that a man does not think the historic Christian faith, which has given him his spiritual nurture, to be worthy of a fair hearing. I am not asking him to close his eyes to what can be said against the historic faith. But, I am telling him that the logical order is to learn what a thing is before one attends exclusively to what can be said against it: and I am telling him further, that the way to learn what a thing is is not to listen first to its opponents, but to grant a full hearing to those who believe in it with all their minds and hearts. After that has been done, after our students, by pursuing the complete course of study, have obtained something like an orderly acquaintance with the marvelous system of truth that the Bible contains, then the more they listen to what can be said against it, the better defenders of it they will probably be.

Let us, therefore, pray that God will raise up for us today true defenders of the Christian faith. We are living in the midst of a mighty conflict against the Christian religion. The conflict is carries on with intellectual weapons. Whether we like it or not, there are millions upon millions of our fellow-men who reject Christianity for the simple reason that they do not believe Christianity to be true. What is to be done in such a situation?

PAST HISTORY OF THE CHURCH

We can learn, at this point, a lesson from the past history of the Church. This is not the first time during the past nineteen hundred years when intellectual objections have been raised against the gospel of Christ. How have those objections been treated? Have they been evaded, or have they been faced? The answer is writ large in the history of the Church. The objections have been faced. God has raised up, in time of need, not only evangelists to appeal to the multitudes, but also Christian scholars to meet the intellectual attack. So it will be in our day, my friends. The Christian religion flourishes not in the darkness but in the light. Intellectual slothfulness is but a quack remedy for unbelief; the true remedy is consecration of intellectual powers to the service of the Lord Jesus Christ.

Let us not fear for the result. Many times, in the course of the past nineteen hundred years, men have predicted that in a generation or so the old gospel would be forever forgotten. Yet the gospel has burst forth again, and set the world aflame. So it may be in our age, in God's good time and in His way. Sad indeed are the substitutes for the gospel of Christ. The Church has been beguiled into By-path Meadow, and is now groaning in the dungeon of Giant Despair. Happy is the man who can point out to such a Church the straight high road that leads over hill and valley to the City of God.

III. THE IMPORTANCE OF CHRISTIAN SCHOLARSHIP FOR THE BUILDING UP OF THE CHURCH

WE HAVE BEEN DISCUSSING today the uses of Christian scholarship. It is important, we showed this morning, for evangelism: it is important, in the second place, as we showed this afternoon, for the defense of the faith. But it has still another use. It is important, in the third place, for the building up of the Church.

THE APOSTOLIC PRACTICE

At this point, as at the first two points, we have the New Testament on our side. At the beginning of the Church's life, as we are told in the Book of Acts, the Apostolic Church continued steadfastly, not

only in fellowship and in breaking of bread and prayers, but also in the apostles' teaching. There is no encouragement whatever, in the New Testament, for the notion that when a man has been converted all has been done for him that needs to be done. Read the Epistles of Paul, in particular, from that point of view. Paul was the greatest of evangelists, and he gloried particularly in preaching the gospel just in places where it had never been heard; yet his Epistles are full of the edification or building up of those who have already been won; and the whole New Testament clearly discourages the exclusive nourishment of Christians with milk instead of with solid food.

DOCTRINAL PREACHING

In the modern Church, this important work of edification has been sadly neglected; it has been neglected even by some of those who believe that the Bible is the Word of God. Too often doctrinal preaching has been pushed from the primary place, in which it rightly belongs, to a secondary place: exhortation has taken the place of systematic instruction; and the people have not been built up. Is it any wonder that a Church thus nurtured is carried away with every wind of doctrine and is helpless in the presence of unbelief? A return to solid instruction in the pulpit, at the desk of the Sunday School teacher, and particularly in the home, is one of the crying needs of the hour.

I do not mean that a sermon should be a lecture; I do not mean that a preacher should address his congregation as a teacher addresses his class. No doubt some young preachers do err in that way. Impressed with the truth that we are trying to present tonight, they have endeavored to instruct the people in Christian doctrine: but in their efforts to be instructive they have put entirely too many points into one sermon and the congregation has been confused. That error, unquestionably, should be avoided. But it should be avoided not by the abandonment of doctrinal preaching, but by our making doctrinal preaching real preaching. The preacher should present to his congregation the doctrine that the Holy Scripture contains; but he should fire the presentation of that doctrine with the devotion of the heart, and he should show how it can be made fruitful for Christian life.

Modern Preaching

One thing that impresses me about preaching today is the neglect of true edification even by evangelical preachers. What the preacher says is often good, and by it genuine Christian emotion is aroused. But a man could sit under the preaching for a year or ten years and at the end of the time he would be just about where he was at the beginning. Such a lamentably small part of Scripture truth is used; the congregation is never made acquainted with the wonderful variety of what the Bible contains. I trust that God may raise up for us preachers of a different type: I trust that those preachers may not only build upon the one foundation which is Jesus Christ, but may build upon that foundation not wood, hay, stubble, but gold, silver, precious stones. Do you, if you are preachers or teachers in the Church, want to be saved merely so as through fire, or do you want your work to endure in the day of Jesus Christ? There is one work at least which I think we may hold, in all humility, to be sure to stand the test of judgment fire; it is the humble impartation, Sunday by Sunday, or day by day, of a solid knowledge not of what you say or what any man has said, but of what God has told us in His Word. Is that work too lowly; is it too restricted to fire the ambition of our souls? Nay, my friends, a hundred lifetimes would not begin to explore the riches of what the Scriptures contain.

What a world in itself the Bible is, my friends! Happy are those who in the providence of God can make the study of it very specifically the business of their lives; but happy also is every Christian who has it open before him and seeks by daily study to penetrate somewhat into the wonderful richness of what it contains.

THE REVELATION OF GOD IN THE BIBLE

A man does not need to read very long in the Bible before that richness begins to appear. It appears in the very first verse of the Bible; for the very first verse sets forth the being of God: "In the beginning God created the heaven and the earth."

We are told today, indeed, that that is metaphysics, and that it is a matter of indifference to the Christian man.[2] That philosophy ought to have been clear from an examination of the universe as it is; the Maker is revealed by the things that He has made. "The Heavens declare the glory of God, and the firmament sheweth His handiwork." "The invisible things of Him from the to be a Christian, it is said, a man does not need at all to settle the question how the universe came into being. The doctrine of "fiat creation," we are told, belongs to philosophy, not to religion; and we can be worshippers of goodness even though

---

[2] With what follows compare the treatment by the lecturer in "What is Faith," 1925. pp. 26-66.

goodness is not clothed with the vulgar trappings of power.

But to talk thus is to talk nonsense, for the simple reason that goodness divorced from power is a mere abstraction which can never call forth the devotion of a man's heart. Goodness inheres only in persons; goodness implies the power to act. Make God good only and not powerful, and you have done away not only with God, but with goodness as well.

Very different from such a pale abstraction, which identifies God with one aspect of the universe, is the God whom the first verse of Genesis presents. That God is the living God; it is He by Whom the worlds were made and by Whom they are upheld.

No, my friends, it is altogether wrong to say that the Christian religion can do perfectly well with many different types of philosophy, and that metaphysical questions are a matter of indifference to the Christian man. Nothing could be farther from the truth. As a matter of fact, everything else that the Bible contains is based upon the stupendous metaphysic that the first verse of Genesis contains. That was the metaphysic of our Lord Jesus Christ, and without it everything that He said and everything that He did would be vain. Underlying all His teaching and all His example is the stupendous recognition that God is the Maker and Ruler of the world: and the Bible from beginning to end depends upon that same "philosophy" of a personal God.

THE REVELATION OF GOD IN NATURE

creation of the world are clearly seen, being understood by the things that are made, even His eternal power and Godhead." Natural religion has, therefore, the full sanction of the Bible: and at the foundation of every theological course should be philosophical apologetics, including the proof of the existence of a personal God, Creator and Ruler of the world.

I know there are those who tell us today that no such study is necessary; there are those who tell us that we should begin with Jesus, and that all we need to know is that God is like Jesus. They talk to us, in that sense, about the "Christlike God." But do you not see that if you relinquish the thought of a personal God, Creator and Ruler of the world, you are dishonoring the teaching of Jesus from beginning to end? Jesus saw in the lilies of the field the weaving of God:

and the man who wipes out of his consciousness the whole wonderful revelation of God in nature, and then says that all that he needs to know is that God is like Jesus, is dishonoring at the very root of His teaching and of His example that same Jesus whom he is purporting to honor and serve.

THE NEED FOR FULLER REVELATION

The existence of a personal God should have been clear to us from the world as it is, but that revelation of God in nature has been obscured by sin, and to recover it and confirm it we need the blessed supernatural revelation that the Scriptures contain. How graciously that revelation is given! When we rise from the reading of the Bible, if we have read with understanding and with faith, what a wonderful knowledge we have of the living God!

In His presence, indeed, we can never lose the sense of wonder. Infinitesimal are the things that we know compared with the things that we do not know; a dreadful curtain veils the being of God from the eyes of man. Yet that curtain, in the infinite goodness of God, has been pulled gently aside, and we have been granted just a look beyond. Never can we cease to wonder in the presence of God: but enough knowledge has been granted to us that we may adore.

THE REVELATION OF MAN IN THE BIBLE

The second great mystery that the Bible presents is the mystery of man. And we are not allowed to wait long for that mystery. It is presented to us, as is the mystery of God, in the early part of the first book of the Bible. Man is there presented in his utter distinctness from the rest of the creation: and then he is presented to us in the awful mystery of his sin.

At that point, it is interesting to observe how the Bible, unlike modern religious literature, always defines its terms: and at the beginning, when the Bible speaks of sin, it makes clear exactly what sin is. According to the Westminster Shorter Catechism, if you will pardon an allusion to that upon which your speaker was brought up, "sin is any want of conformity unto, or transgression of the law of God." I do not remember, at the moment, what proof-texts the authors of the Westminster Standards used to support that definition. But they need hardly have looked farther for such proof-texts than to the early part of Genesis. "Ye shall not eat of the tree," said God: man ate of the tree and died. Sin is there presented with the utmost clearness as the transgression of law. So it is presented in the whole of the Bible. Sin and law belong together. When we say "sin" we have said "law": when we have said "law," then, man being what he now is, we have said "sin."

At the present time, the existence of law is being denied. Men no longer believe that there is such a thing as a law of God; and naturally they do not believe that there is such a thing as sin. Thoughtful men, who are not Christians, are aware of the problem that this stupendous change in human thinking presents to the modern world. Now that men no longer believe that there is a law of God, now that men no longer believe in obligatory morality, now that the moral law has been abandoned, what is to be put in its place, in order that an ordinarily decent human life may be preserved upon the earth? It cannot be said that the answers proposed for that question are as satisfactory as the way in which the question itself is put. It is impossible to keep back the raging seas of human passion with the flimsy mud embankments of an appeal either to self interest, or to what Walter Lippmann calls "disinterestedness." Those raging seas can only be checked by the solid masonry of the law of God.

WHAT IS WRONG WITH THE WORLD?

Men are wondering today what is wrong with the world. They are conscious of the fact that they are standing over some terrible abyss. Awful ebullitions rise from that abyss. We have lost altogether the sense of the security of our Western civilization. Men are wondering what is wrong.

It is perfectly clear what is wrong. The law of God has been torn up, as though it were a scrap of paper, and the inevitable result is appearing with ever greater clearness. When will the law be rediscovered? When it is re-discovered, that will be a day of terror for mankind: but it will also be a day of joy; for the law will be a schoolmaster unto Christ. Its terrors will drive men back to the little wicket gate, and to the way that leads to that place somewhat ascending where they will see the Cross.

Those are the two great presuppositions of everything else that the Bible contains; the two great presuppositions are the majesty of the transcendent God and the guilt and misery of man in his sin. But we are not left to wait long for the third of the great mysteries–the mystery of salvation. That, too, is presented at the beginning of Genesis, in the promise of a redemption to come.

The rest of the Bible is the unfolding of that promise. And when I think of that unfolding, when I try to take the Bible, not in part, but as a whole, when I contemplate not this doctrine or that, but the marvelous system of doctrine that the Bible contains, I am amazed that in the presence of such riches men can be content with that other gospel which now dominates the preaching in the Church.

THE GOSPEL UNFOLDED IN SCRIPTURE

When I think again of the wonderful metaphysic in the first verse of Genesis–"In the beginning God created the heaven and the earth"–when I think of the way in which throughout the Old Testament the majesty of that Creator God is presented with wonderful clearness, until the presentation culminates in the matchless fortieth chapter of Isaiah–"It is He that sitteth upon the circle of the earth, and the inhabitants thereof are as grasshoppers, that stretcheth out the heavens as a curtain, and spreadeth them out as a tent to dwell in"–when I think of the way in which in that same chapter the tenderness and the gentleness of that same awful God are represented, in a manner far beyond all human imagining–"He shall feed His flock like a shepherd: He shall gather the lambs with His arm, and carry them in His bosom, and shall gently lead those that are with young"– when I think of the wonderful gallery of portraits in the Old Testament, and compare it with the best efforts of men who have sought to penetrate into the secrets of human life and of the human heart: when I think of the gracious dealings of God with His people in Old Testament times, until the fullness of the time was come, and the Savior was born into the world: when I think of the way in which His coming was accomplished, by a stupendous miracle indeed, but in wonderful quietness and lowliness; when I think of the songs of the heavenly host, and the way in which the infant Savior was greeted in the Temple by those who had waited for the redemption of Jerusalem; when I stand in awe before that strange answer of the youthful Jesus, "Wist ye not that I must be about My Father's business?"; when I try to keep my imagination at rest, as Scripture bids me do, regarding those

long, silent years at Nazareth; when I think of the
day of His showing to Israel; when I think of the
sternness of His teaching, the way in which He
pulled the cloak from human sin, the way in
which, by revealing through His words and His
example the real demands of God, He took from
mankind its last hope of any salvation to be
obtained through its own goodness; when I think
again of the wonderful kindness of the Savior;
when I read how He forgave where none other
would forgive, and helped where all other helpers
had failed; when I think, above all, of that blessed
thing which He did not only for men of long
ago, who saw Him with their bodily eyes, but for
every one of us if we be united with Him through
faith, when He died in our stead upon the Cross,
and said in triumph, at the moment when His
redeeming work was done, "It is finished"; when
I enter into both the fear and the joy of those
who found the tomb empty and saw the vision
of angels which also said, "He is not here: for He
is risen"; when I think of the way in which He
was known to His disciples in the breaking of
bread; when I think of Pentecost and the pouring
out of His Spirit upon the Church; when I
attend to the wonderful way in which the Bible
tells us how this Savior may be our Savior today,

how you and I, sitting in this house to-night, can come into His presence, in even far more intimate fashion than that which was enjoyed by those who pushed their way unto Him as He sat amidst scribes and Pharisees when He was on earth; when I think of the application of His redeeming work by the Holy Spirit: "Be of sin the double cure. Cleanse me from its guilt and power"; when I think of the glories of the Christian life, opened to us, not on the basis of human striving, but of that mighty act of God; when I read the last book of the Bible, and think of the unfolding of the glorious hope of that time when the once lowly Jesus, now seated on the throne of all being, shall come again with power– when I think of these things, I am impressed with the fact that the other gospel, which is dominant in the Church today, preached though it is by brilliant men, and admirable though it might have seemed if we had not compared it with something infinitely greater, is naught but "weak and beggarly elements," and that the humblest man who believes that the Bible is the Word of God is possessed of riches greater by far than all the learning of all the world and all the eloquence of all the preachers who now have the ear of an unfaithful Church.

36573999R00037

Printed in Great Britain
by Amazon